Mixing Mu...

Written by Emma Lynch

I am peckish.

I am mixing muffins.

This is my list of jobs.
1. Dip my hands in the suds.

2. Get Mum. She must click
this on. It gets hot.

3. Get a mixing dish. No rushing!

4. Mix the things in the dish.

5. Mix in a pinch of this.

6. Mix in the choc chips.

7. Drench with milk and eggs.

The mix is frothing!

8. I must not spill the
muffin mix.

I am longing to lick the dish!

9. Mum must get the muffins.
They will be hot.

10. Dip the things in the suds.

I am longing to test the muffins. Tuck in, Mum!